Finding Hope in the Midst of Grief

A Practical Spiritual Guide to Dealing with the Loss of a Spouse

2nd Edition

~

A book by: Judy St. Pierre

© 2020 Finding Hope In The Midst Of Grief
All Rights Reserved.

No part of this book may be reproduced, stored in a retrieval system, or transmitted by any means without the written permission of the author.

Published by Word Therapy Publishing
December 16, 2020

ISBN-13: 978-1-7361111-0-9

Printed in the United States of America all rights reserved under international Copyright laws.

Cover Design by: Aspen Denita

Word Therapy Publishing, LLC
P.O. Box 939
Hope Mills, NC 28348
www.wordtherapypublishing.com

Any people depicted in stock imagery provided by Thinkstock are models, and such images are being used for illustrative purposes only. All other photos were printed with permission from the owner or are public domain.

Because of the dynamic nature of the Internet, any web addresses or links contained in this book may have changed since publication and may no longer be valid. The views expressed in this work are solely those of the author and do not necessarily reflect the views of the publisher, and the publisher hereby disclaims any responsibility for them.

~ Dedication ~

I am dedicating this book to my sister Joy Nolen. I am so thankful God has put you in my life. Together we have seen God's provision in all we have been through together. I love you Sis!

- Judy

~ Acknowledgements ~

God bless all who read this book. My hope is that it will bring you hope and guidance as you start your life over. Please know that you, as a reader of this book, are being covered in prayer daily. May God's peace and the comfort of the Holy Spirit be with you every moment of every day.

~Judy

Table of Contents

Chapter 1: We Never Plan to Grieve

Chapter 2: You Can Be Productive and Grieve

Chapter 3: Give Yourself Permission to Heal Your Way

Chapter 4: Alone and Feeling Hurt

Chapter 5: KNOW That Your Feelings Are Valid

Chapter 6: There Is No Standard Time Limit for Grief

Chapter 7: The Journey of Grief is NOT a Straight Line

Chapter 8: Your Relationship With the Person You Lost Significantly Impacts Your Response to God During the Grieving Process

Chapter 9: Grief Doesn't Take the Day Off for Holidays, Family Gatherings, and Special Occasions

Chapter 10: Additional Tools for When Anger and Guilt Resurface

Chapter 11: When the Unknown Comes to Light

Chapter 12: Don't Fear Grief; Just do the Work to Heal

Chapter 1: We Never Plan to Grieve

We all have moments in our lives.

You know what I mean, right?

It's those memorable times that are the culmination of planning, praying, and hoping that something special and amazing happens in our lives. Those times are so much more than memories, they are moments.

When I was planning for my wedding, I hoped and prayed for the most beautiful experience imaginable. This meant months, weeks, and days of planning right up until the very last minute possible.

To be honest, I can remember everything that happened all the way up until we both said, "I do."

My journey to that moment started as I was working fulltime and balancing 19 credits in school. The goal was to finish up the semester so I could focus on our big day. January 9th, 1982 was the day we had set aside specifically to fill with unforgettable moments.

Even as I write these words, I still remember how nervous and excited I was at the same time. I remember the sound my dress made as I walked down the aisle to my soon to be husband.

I will never forget how, at the moment we kneeled for prayer, we heard the echoing of stifled laughter because someone had written "Help Me" on the bottom of Jerry's shoes.

We didn't plan that moment, but it is forever etched in our memories.

And of course who could forget taking those vows.

Promising to love, honor, and obey, in sickness and in health…

And who could forget, 'till death do us part."

As I said those words that day, like so many others have, I didn't fully understand the weight of that declaration.

I didn't think about the impact of being separated from this person I love by death.

But that not only became my reality, but my new normal. And sadly, it is the story of so many.

In fact, many of us who fondly reflect on our wedding day find ourselves wondering, not just what is next for us, but can we really go on without our spouse.

Our definition and understanding of happiness had been linked to moments and memories we shared with our loved ones, and now, we're not even sure we will ever be happy again.

And we are now facing the challenging realization that our spouses are not coming back to us.

Not to mention what that actually means for life as we know it.

We have the realization that we will be raising children on our own.

Meanwhile, our friends and family are moving on with their lives as if nothing ever happened.

As if they don't know we've lost the love of our life.

And we even question what's next for us.

I remember 3 weeks before my husband Jerry died, we were eating dinner, and he asked me, "What would you do if I died?" At the time, my mind could not even comprehend such a thought, and I told him I didn't want to talk or even think about that.

But he was persistent and wanted an answer.

So, I casually mentioned the kids and I would go back to Newhall and I would finish up my degree; but after that, I did not know what I would do. My answer seemed acceptable to him, and nothing else was said about the subject.

Were it not for this conversation before my husband actually died, I would not have had a starting point when the "what if" became a reality. Now I had at least some direction for life, for me, and for the kids.

But that's who Jerry was.

He was the middle child of 7 kids. He had three older brothers and three younger sisters. He was born and grew up in Indiana. He was in the Air force for 5 years before coming to college.

For me, he was 6'2" with blue eyes, and I thought he was a cutie!

When we met on the first day of college, I never would have imagined the journey we would embark upon. But I can say, when he first walked into that room, my first thought was, "baby, you are mine."

And that led to us dating for 2 ½ years before we got married.

During our time together I learned so much about Jerry. Like the fact that he was a spiritual leader, and made every effort to ensure that we had a Christ-centered relationship prior to being married. He even led us in bible study and daily prayer frequently when we were dating and also when we were married.

The fact that he always put Jesus first in his life drew me even closer to him during our time together.

Not to mention the fact that he was a gentleman who believed in opening doors for me, pulling out my chair at dinner, etc.

And he was very much the leader of our family.

We had family devotionals almost every night in which he would lead, and we always closed the evening in prayer. He started a tradition, shortly after we were married, that he called "wisdom time". And during this "wisdom time" we would share various issues we may have faced that day. It was a time that we could bring things to the table, like if we'd upset each other or struggled with something throughout the day. This would prove to be invaluable to our relationship and me as an individual.

Jerry led our family through these moments and memories, and even today, we all benefit from the many practical principles and lessons he laid the foundation for. This holds true for my son, Nathaniel, who was just 5 months old, and my daughter, Elicia, who was 18 months old when Jerry passed.

So when I think back to that simple conversation that Jerry started about planning to live, survive, and thrive should he not be there, I am even more grateful for his leadership and foresight for our family.

And even though I can see the benefit of so many things today, the journey through grief to get to this point was not easy. It wasn't a straight line like the textbooks say, it was riddled with ups, downs and major curves along the way.

And that's what I want to help you to see as you read the lessons and stories I share.

Grief is an inevitable process. It is well defined and documented by some of the greatest minds of the world. And even with all that insight and education on the subject, it can be a scary, isolating, and emotionally exhausting process that is specific to each individual person.

And you know what… that's OK. The goal isn't to check the stages of grief off of some list. The goal is to navigate your grief path in a way that makes sense to you and leads to your healing and wholeness.

Chapter 2: You Can Be Productive and Grieve

Making the transition from living your life with your loved one to not having them is more than a little challenging. We plan for some of the biggest moments in our lives, but losing loved ones and dealing with the grief that follows is not usually one of them.

But did you know that even in the midst of grief and all that entails, you can be productive?

It's true.

Despite the myriad of emotions, despite the spiritual and emotional battles that you face on any given day and despite the sudden realization that you are now considered "single," this time in your life has a purpose.

Before we dig into this, let's take some time to really define what grief and being productive look like.

To put it simply, "grief is a loss we experience that causes deep sorrow of some kind," and "being productive is having the quality or power of producing in abundance."

With this in mind, here's how we can be productive in multiple areas of our lives, even as we grieve.

As you move through the grieving process, it can be very easy to shut down and stop doing so many things simply because you are consumed by the loss.

Let's face it, the loss of your spouse is something that you carry with you throughout every day, so in addition to finding the strength and energy to care for the kids and take care of the house and other responsibilities, you will have days when you struggle to get out of bed.

It can be so overwhelming that we feel we will never be able to accomplish anything again.

The key to combat this is to start small. Try to focus on some simple self care for yourself, like preparing a simple breakfast, or getting your juices flowing by going to the mailbox daily.

While those are simple personal tasks you can tackle, you may also be faced with returning to work after your loss. This can be a very challenging time, and work is a place where you are expected to leave your personal challenges at the door. So if you are returning to work, it can be very helpful to organize the tasks of your day based on priority. That means not just listing everything that needs to be done, but listing them in the order that they can be completed, then going a step further and setting timed deadlines for each task. This will help you not only tackle your work, but also help you keep things in perspective as you grieve.

And for those of us who don't work outside of the home, continuing to operate and raise kids in the home you had built with your spouse can be very difficult. So the way that you remain productive in the home is to set a schedule so that you are consistently feeding the children, helping them to get ready for school, and doing things to provide for their needs.

While this does not eliminate grief, it does ensure that you don't pile guilt onto your grief because those who need you (i.e., work or kids) are still being addressed as you process your grief.

Please know that during this time, you will consistently feel a myriad of emotions. You may often feel like you are just going through the motions; you may feel mad at your spouse for dying; you may feel tired and discouraged. And these emotions are all part of the process.

When I found myself in this rollercoaster ride of emotions, I felt like I was the only one who had ever felt this way, until I started opening up and communicating with friends who had similar losses. And once we started sharing, we all realized that we were dealing with how challenging the loss was for each of us and that there was some anger there.

In this instance, communication was very productive, and this is something for you to remember as you navigate grief. Find a safe space that you can communicate throughout this process. Notice that it may not be friends or family if they have not experienced the loss of a spouse, but it may be a church group or other support group for those who have lost their loved ones.

Suffering in silence is NOT productive.

Having that outlet can not only be productive, but it can help you to be better prepared to deal with your day to day responsibilities as well as interact with others. This can keep you from venting to a co-worker who asks how you're doing because you have a healthy outlet where you feel heard, because remember, not everyone at work needs to know or can relate to the deep pain you're feeling.

Having a designated outlet to share your true feelings with can really help in this process. And if you are struggling to be present and productive in your day to day life following the loss of your spouse, don't burden yourself to push through alone. Take steps to ease the pressure.

- Check with your employer to see if there are leave or extended leave options available to you.
- If financially feasible, ask your employer for reduced hours or extended lunch options to help you combat overwhelm.
- Seek out daycare or special activities for the kids to attend regularly.
- Ask friends or relatives, to sit with the kids 1 or 2 days a week so that you can work on your healing.

These are just a few suggestions, but if you find yourself overwhelmed by the responsibilities of home or work, feeling like you have no outlet or time to deal with your grief, things are piling up all around you, find something that works for you. There is no shame in asking for help and thinking of your needs during this time. In fact, support and self-care are two staples that will help you to heal and maintain some semblance of normalcy during this time. And even if you find that you are unable to return to work, or need to change things around your home, it's ok. God knows your needs and may have a different job for you to go to or another option for you to run your home.

As I went through this when Jerry died, I was so overwhelmed with grief, I did not think I would ever be able to function, care for the house, or do anything productive again.

To be honest, I was in complete denial that my husband was even gone. However, because my kids were so small, they depended completely on me, so I stayed busy. And even in the midst of my busyness, I didn't want to go on.

I share this because some of you feel this deep down inside also.

But know that during these deep times of grief, God understands our heart. It may be all we can do to just get through the day, so I would encourage you as you seek God through prayer and His word, that you be honest with him. Because he knows how you are feeling anyway. Know that in the midst of your grief, you may not be productive in all areas of your life.

Take it a day at a time.

Throughout your days, speak out loud to God about what areas you need help in. An example of this would be "Lord Jesus, I know I have to get up and get things going for my kids. I don't even want to get out of bed. But with your help, Jesus, I can do this." You may not feel it but get up and do it. God will honor your prayer. Thank him for his providence in your life. God loves you so much. Look up Hebrews 4:16

It can be so easy when we are around others to be persuaded that we need to grieve a certain way, or how others think we should. But this is not so! God knows our needs and will help us with our healing his way. But this is still hard to deal with, so in our next chapter, we will be digging into how to give yourself permission to heal your way.

Chapter 3: Give Yourself Permission to Heal Your Way

When we're grieving, one of the most challenging things is dealing with the cliché and well-meaning quotes from others. In fact, more often than not, the last thing we want or need is to have someone telling us things like "you'll get over it." Or even quoting something like, "And we know that all things work together for good for those who love God and are called according to his purpose," (Romans 8:28).

And I will never forget when someone said to me, "you will be surprised how quickly you will get over it," when Jerry died. (I was shocked. I mean seriously, my husband just died, and you opt to tell me that!)

No matter the words or even the intent of the person delivering them, it's easy to understand why they come off as insensitive and rude. And I'm quite sure that you've also been on the receiving end of one of these remarks too. Unfortunately, these remarks people offer are to make them feel better instead of to comfort us.

In these times, it's best to focus on what you need for healthy grieving and make the decision to just walk away from this person because they are only adding to our pain and grief.

The goal is to find the best and most healthy ways for us to heal AND continue to function in our lives. Sometimes, this will lead to those around us feeling unappreciated or not understanding our want and need to walk away from certain situations, and that's ok. Simply make the person aware that you love/like them, but for now, you need to have some time to yourself if that's what is needed.

With this, it is important to know that as we are grieving, there may be times when we are getting better and then revert to a painful or emotional state of grieving. So conversations and interactions you were able to tolerate just last week may trigger you or upset you this week. This is normal, so you must allow yourself to grieve and not try to suppress emotions and feelings. Please also note that some close friends, or perhaps even family members, may distance themselves during your time of grief, and this is also normal and has less to do with you or their love for you but, in most cases, they just find it difficult to be present during your grief journey. They feel uncertain or uncomfortable as they don't know what to do, say, or even what role they play as you work to heal.

Remember to be selective about who you share your pain/grieving with. God has given us close friends that will be with us through it all. I was lucky enough to have two very close friends in the early stages of my grief. At times these two friends cried with me. Romans 12:15 says, "Rejoice with those who rejoice and weep with those who weep". My two friends showed this type of compassion with me. Hang on to those who are with you in your grief. Talk to your pastor to obtain help if you don't have anyone in your life like this. Pray for God to bring people into your life to help.

So, how do you give yourself permission to grieve AND handle the expectations of others in the process?

Through your journey, you will have to give yourself permission to grieve in a way that feels true to you, several times over. And guess what? It won't always fit into what others consider grieving.

One example of this for me was actually on the day of Jerry's funeral. The calendar displayed July 16, 1984, but I assure you it is a day I will never forget.

Jerry's sister came in and said, "Good morning, time to get up and ready for the big day!"

Her statement took my breath away.

She acted as if we were preparing for a birthday, graduation, or some other joyous occasion. I had quite a few things I would have liked to tell her, but I didn't. I swallowed my grief and went about the day as best I could.

I can honestly say that I wasn't prepared for everyone to be smiling and laughing. But there they were acting as if this was just another family gathering. But to me, it was deeper than that. It was a representation that they did NOT feel any loss over Jerry's death. They all seemed fine, and I felt like I was missing a part of myself.

I felt even more isolated and alone.

By the time we got to the funeral I wanted to cry but couldn't. I almost felt like by grieving openly, I would bring everyone else's good mood down. At one point, I even felt like I was playing the role of a widow in a movie scene. Then when it was finally time to leave, I broke down and cried because I didn't want to leave him.

Then the thing I feared happened.

My grief was on display and others thought it was unacceptable.

As I wept, I felt a firm grasp on my arm, and I was led back to the car.

Some of you may have gone through similar situations where your family and friends were trying to be helpful at the funeral. Perhaps those around you at this time may have come off as rude and uncaring in their remarks and actions. Please know that your feelings of frustration and anger are indeed normal, and they are valid. How you feel during this time is just that, how you feel. There is no right or wrong answer, and no one can tell you how to feel. Understanding, accepting, and giving yourself permission to fully grieve will also help you to deal with and respond to those around you who don't understand.

At times when they say rude things, you can either just walk away or confront them by saying, "that remark was not helpful at all to me. As a matter of fact, it hurt my feelings deeply." They may apologize or perhaps just walk away from you. Like we talked about earlier in this chapter, each one of us grieves in a different manner. In our grieving, we might take 5 steps forward and then 3 or 4 steps backward. This is normal. Don't be hard on yourself if you have gone through this, or you may go through this in the future.

Don't try and share with everyone about your grieving. It is ok when someone asks you how you are doing to say, "I am fine, thank you." Or even, "I am ok; please keep praying for me". Know that others around you, as I mentioned earlier, may not understand what you are going through. They may be trying to help you but just make you feel worse. In summary, I had several friends that my husband and I knew together that were not able to be around me when I was grieving. Some of the wives felt threatened, as if I were going to take their husbands away from them. Of course, nothing like this ever crossed my mind. I also had many single friends that walked away from me because of my grief. So, it was very hard for me at times. Please realize that it may be hard on you also.

God has not set a time limit on your grief. Each person will be different. But God will be with you as long as it takes. Don't worry, and try not to focus on what others are telling you about your grief. Remember this verse, Hebrews 4:16 "Let us then approach God's throne of grace with confidence, so that we may receive mercy and find grace to help us in our time of need".

We have covered a lot about grieving our own way and the reactions of others in our lives as we grieve. The pain can be overwhelming. We can and will experience emotions that we are not sure how to handle. While we are allowing ourselves to grieve, it is important that we take care of ourselves. It is important to try and get sleep. However, for some, it may be hard to sleep at different times. It is also important to try and eat healthy foods so we have the energy to deal with the areas of our life that will be harder to deal with during this time period of our grief. Realize once again that there is no right or wrong way to grieve. Grieving is dependent on many factors. It could depend on your life experience, your faith/walk with God. Take each day one at a time. At times it is by the hour or even by the minute. Grieving for a loss is not easy. So, be kind to yourself. Consider starting a journal and really focusing on the many ways that God is answering our call and helping us. We can then look back and realize and see God's faithfulness in times of grief where we feel there is no way out.

In our next chapter we're going to be focusing more on understanding that our feelings are valid and further discussing the fact that there is no timeframe for grieving. Even if we have a family member and/or someone from our church tell us that we have been grieving long enough.

Chapter 4: Alone and Feeling Hurt

We all have important things that happen in our lives. Of course, my wedding day was filled with moments that I will never forget, and with that, I will never forget taking the vow 'Till death do us part". When I said this vow, I truly believed that my husband and I would have 50 or 60 years together before we were separated by death.

Sadly, that was not the case as my husband passed away after just 2 1/2 years of marriage.

As you read this, you may reflect on that same vow, and whether you were together for a longer or shorter period of time. The fact is, our spouses are no longer with us, and we now have to proceed with our life without them. It's normal to feel overwhelmed because we are not sure how we are going to handle life on our own. We wonder if we can enjoy life again. What is next in our life? Is it wrong for me to want to be happy again? These kinds of questions are normal when you've lost a loved one.

Yes, we will enjoy life again, but it will take some time.

It's hard in the beginning as we watch people go on with their lives while we basically exist in a suspended state in our own lives. Others are growing, moving on, setting goals, and reaching goals, and we are trying to get to a place where we can simply smile or laugh.

It's normal to feel like it's not right for others to go on as if your loved one never existed. It's also normal to feel like people simply don't know that we have lost the most important person in our lives.

Watching others go on with their lives was almost as difficult as the day I found out that Jerry had died. I had no energy to do anything.

Even now, I remember it like it was yesterday. Jerry called me at about 5:45 pm, letting me know that he had gone to the hospital because his eye was hurting a lot. I was more than a little concerned, and of course I shared that with him, but he said he had been given medication and was on his way home.

He let me know that he would be home soon and I told him I loved him and would see him when he got home. He replied that he loved me, too, and would see me when he got home.

Those were our last words to each other.

Hours passed, and he still hadn't made it home yet, so I had a neighbor drive me to the base using the route I knew Jerry always took to the Air Force Base. At the time we were stationed in England, so as the neighbor drove, I was looking everywhere along the roads just in case Jerry might have pulled off to the side of the road to rest.

Once we got to the base and made it to the officers club, I overheard someone talking about the death of someone who lived in Oxford (where we lived).

Somehow I knew they were talking about my Jerry.

I let the Officers know that my husband and I were from Oxford, and he had not come home yet. They asked for my military card and then asked me to wait in a room. As I sat there waiting for answers, information, or anything, it seemed like hours. But in reality, it was only about 45 minutes.

When the officers came into the room, they told me to sit down and then delivered a blow that changed my life forever.

"Mrs. St. Pierre, we found your husband dead in his car tonight. We believe he had a mild heart attack."

I didn't believe them. I couldn't. Because if I did, that meant that the person I was supposed to navigate life with was gone.

The grief started instantly, and at that moment, I was in denial.

While your story may be different, you may be able to relate to my feelings around losing Jerry, and if the loss was sudden or unexpected, it is normal to have feelings of not wanting to move on, right away anyway.

I encourage you to share the details of your spouse's passing. It will help you later as you are able to reflect back and see how God has brought you through. Now, as we reflect on first hearing the news of the death, we think about "How can I go on?" Here are three things that will be important to take care of yourself.

1. Look after your health. When we are dealing with such things as grief, it is paramount that we take good care of our health. This will not always be easy. But our bodies are going through internal turmoil.
2. Get plenty of rest and sleep.
3. Avoid making major life decisions in the early stages of grief.

Over a period of time, you will be happy again. However, it may not be easy. You may not even want to get out of bed. Here are a few suggestions for you.

Make a list daily of things you would like to accomplish.

Make the list very practical.

Example:
1. Make bed.
2. Cook breakfast.
3. Go for a walk.

Crossing each item off the list once you have accomplished it. I would encourage you to keep a daily journal. Write your feelings out.

Being able to talk about it will help. It is not good or healthy to keep your feelings repressed. Also, you may not have anyone that will allow you to talk about it, so keeping a journal is helpful. You will be able to use your journal as a means of looking back and seeing yourself being productive. This will be useful in knowing you are getting things done.

Give yourself permission to not have to finish everything that is on your daily list. At the end of the day you will be able to see, by looking at your list, that you are being productive, but remember not to be too hard on yourself if you don't accomplish everything on the list. We talked earlier about being happy again, but in the early stages of grief it is normal to feel overwhelmed.

Something else I encourage you to do is memorize the following verses Hebrews 4:16 "Let us then approach God's throne of grace with confidence, so that we may receive mercy and find grace to help us in our time of need" and I Peter 5:7 "casting all ty care upon him for he careth for you."

When you have thoughts that are weighing you down, these verses may help you. I would encourage you to look up other verses and put them down in your journal. Reflect back on them as you need to. God loves us and will be with us at all times. You may not feel God's love because of the pain you are going through, however, rely on the truth. A simple prayer, "God, I am hurting so deeply right now. I don't feel your love or presence, but I am standing on your word that I know is true." You will get through this. The next step of our journey will be dealing with being productive while we are grieving. It is possible. Let's go to the next chapter and tackle this together.

Chapter 5: KNOW That Your Feelings Are Valid

Repressing feelings, thoughts, and sometimes our words can become a painful habit while we are grieving. But the key to moving out of this space is to really be sure that we know and understand that how we feel, and the thoughts we have, are valid. In fact, not only does denying our feelings over long periods of time extend the grieving process, but it can also result in new emotional challenges and issues because of continued suppression or repression.

One symptom or behavior that may be displayed as a result of not validating our feelings is an increase in hostility in our lives. Displaying hostility doesn't mean you're a bad person. It can actually be the result of multiple triggers or issues. And for those who are grieving, the root of the issue is most often due to a sudden change and inability to live life in the same way you have in the past.

Anger is another outward display that can be the result of repressed feelings. During times of grief, it is very easy to find yourself lashing out at friends and family members for the smallest things. And as much as we need the love and support of others, this can cause friends and family to not want to be around us during this time, which is very understandable as even those who have been kind to us in our grief can become easy targets of our displays of anger.

Even if our usual demeanor is cheerful and happy, or friends and family regard us as being quick to help others, during this time, those same friends and family may be really caught off guard by the sharp change in demeanor brought on by grief and holding in our feelings. They may even go as far as to say that we are hard to be around.

With so much going on internally and around us, it can be very easy to take on an "I don't care" attitude.

But of course, beneath all the hurt, anger, and other emotions, we really do care. Because there is no right or wrong way we are supposed to feel. We need to realize this. At times we may feel alone like no one cares.

We bury our sadness and grief so we can appear radiant! There is nothing at all wrong with us is what we want people to believe. We want to be accepted with those in our Christian circle. We must keep our lives in such a way that it can be said, "Look at Judy. She just lost her spouse, and she is so happy. She is reading her bible every day and praying to God. We can tell that she is really trusting God through all of this." In most cases, I would say that statement is only a dream.

However, we all grieve in different ways.

How long we go through various cycles of a loss will be different for each of us. I do know that God is with us through all of this. He knows we are hurt, missing our spouse, and having issues dealing with different areas. I would encourage you to seek God in all of this. Be honest with him. He knows how you are feeling anyway. A verse that has been very precious to me when I have felt low is Hebrews 4:16 "Therefore let us confidently approach the throne of grace with boldness, so that we may receive mercy and find grace to help us at the proper time."

We need to learn how to deal with loss. How we react to failure or grief in our lives is a major part of the journey we are going through. I know that the one major thing that

God told me that I needed to deal with is forgiveness toward my stepdad. My stepdad told me every day of my life
"You will never amount to one G-D thing." I remember one time I looked him in the eye and said "Oh, yes, I will." He got so angry. His words controlled my life for years. I recall when I was studying for my teaching credential that when I took one of the exams, I did not pass. I was ready to just give up. My friend, Faith, looked at me and said, "How much longer are you going to let Bob, control what you think and do? Take the test again, pass it, and prove him wrong." Bob, my stepfather, was never very supportive of me. Is there someone in your life that you need to forgive? Please read this part very carefully several times if you need to.

FORGIVENESS IS FOR YOU, NOT FOR THE PERSON THAT HURT YOU. FORGIVENESS IS FOR YOU!

Please understand when we forgive someone, that does not mean we forget. With God's grace, the hurt will diminish as time passes. I can say my stepfather no longer has a hold on my life. I have been set free, and it has been wonderful. God can do the same for you with any relationship in your life. We will have issues that we need to deal with. A major issue that I had was that we are not weak as we deal with our emotions. Allow yourself to grieve as so needed. There will, of course, be times when you may have to say to yourself. Ok, I am feeling this way right now and will deal with it later. An example would be my career of being a teacher. When you have over 30 – 5 and 6-year-olds in a room, you keep quite busy. Let's talk about some ways to validate your feelings. One important way to do this is to decide NOT to suppress your feelings just to make others happy. However, when people ask you how you are doing, it is ok to say, "Hi, I am ok, thank you" or a simple "ok." I would not encourage you to tell everyone exactly how you are doing. As a matter of fact, when people ask you how you are doing, in reality, they are only asking to be polite.

Keep how you are truly feeling to a select few. I would also encourage you to go back to your journal writing. Write down how your feeling. Keep track of all your prayer requests and the dates you have entered into your journal when your prayers have been answered. When you have days that are hard to feel God's presence, you will be able to go back to your journal writing and see how God indeed has answered prayers. When we go through anger that we can't control, a good way of dealing with this is to put yourself in a short time out. For example, if the person you are angry at is in the same room as you. Being angry at your spouse and or God for leaving you alone is very real. Think about the cause of your anger. Mine was anger towards my husband, Jerry, and at God that my spouse was no longer with me. Being angry is not a sin. Let's look at a verse in the bible that deals with this Ephesians 4:26 "In your anger do not sin...Do not let the sun go down while you are still angry." It is ok to be angry. However, God does want us.

How we deal with anger can come out in different ways depending on each individual. For some people, like me, it can cause physical stress. Stress, like losing our spouse, will affect our health, job, and how we relate to our friends and family. Like I mentioned early, stress/grief can cause us to be angry, hostile, and various other reactions. It is important that you do have someone in your life that you are able to go and talk to. If you know Jesus as your personal savior and Lord, you are still going to go through the emotions from losing your spouse. But, we have an amazing verse to look to, John 14:1, "Let not your heart be troubled. Believe in God; believe also in me." In our loss we desperately need God. He is the only one that can give us the things we need to cope with our loss. I will stop here and say that there was a period of time when I wanted nothing to do with God. I was so angry with him. You might have gone through this also. As a matter of fact, you may be in a position where you are mad right now. Let God know how mad you are. Be honest with him as to how you are feeling. Let me say something I think is important. Believing in God does not mean we will have and live a life that is completely stress-free. Believing in something or someone leads us to being able to trust. Proverbs 3:6-7 says, "Trust in the Lord with all thine heart and lean not unto thine own understanding, in all thy ways acknowledge him and he will lead your paths."

Another verse for a Christian who is going through a struggle is Philippians 4:6-7 "Do not be anxious about anything, but in every situation, by prayer and petition, with thanksgiving, present your requests to God....7. And the peace of God, which transcends all understanding, will guard your hearts and your minds in Christ Jesus." We have covered a lot here. The one thing above all other I would like to share is, please do not repress your anger. I went around playing the "happy little Christian" for about 5 years. It went on to the point that I did not want to live anymore. I put myself in a Christian program where I was safe. I had two young children, and I knew that I needed to be around for them. So much went on during this time period. It was here that my life was totally transformed. Yes, a few people told me how stupid I was for going into this program. I was not trusting God. One person told me, "Jerry did not belong to you," and therefore, my lack of trust in Jesus was a strong image of how I was a horrible Christian.

People will say mean things to us. They will say things to us to hurt us and perhaps cause us to be angry. Hang on to those friends that are with you through thick and thin.

It was not a lack of trust that made me go into the inpatient Christian program. Some people may try and make you feel low and tell you that your lack of faith is wrong. Do not listen to them. They are not the ones dealing with the loss, you are.

It is also a good idea to join a support group for bereavement because it puts you in a place with those who truly understand and can connect with what you are feeling and going through. In addition to this support from others, it is very important that you know, God will be with you in your grief for as long as it takes. He has not limited you to a certain amount of time to grieve, and because he loves you so much, He wants you to be comforted even more during this time.

I encourage you to keep a daily journal about your feelings. This will be a way of you being able to keep track of how your feeling. It also gives an account of how God has been working in your life. It would be a good idea to memorize a few verses on trusting God. I found it helpful to quote Hebrews 4:16 out loud or in my mind if other people were in the room. This is a way of counteracting the pain of some of the things you are dealing with. No, it may not take away the pain, but it indicates that God in control whether we feel like He is or not. We are acting on what we know to be true and not relying on what we feel to be true. So, be honest about how you are feeling with others. (only a few select people). Always be honest with God about how you feel because he knows it. Seek outside help of a one-on-one counselor if needed and/or a bereavement support group. In our next chapter, we will be dealing with the fact that God does not have a time frame for our grief process.

Chapter 6: There Is No Standard Time Limit for Grief.

Grieving is a unique experience, and each person has to deal with it in one form or another during a lifetime. No two people with grief the same way. When we discuss how long the grieving process should be, we will undoubtedly come across several different opinions. As noted earlier, there is no time frame for despair, and with this in mind, it can be really hard to deal with family and friends who think we've grieved enough. A lot of individuals make very insensitive remarks when we are grieving, for instance, the one that really hurt and upset me was: " Get on with your life. Jerry did not belong to you." I'm sure you've also encountered some of these rude and insensitive remarks. But the thing to remember is the person likely did not intend to hurt you with their words. In most instances, while the delivery failed, they were trying to administer words to make us feel better.

As we deepen our discussion on what grieving looks like, I can't help but remember a piece of writing of mine from years ago that read:

God is going to be with me in my grief as long as it takes. He has not set down a law saying, "Only one year, and that is all". He wants me to come to him with my hurts and grief. It was interesting to find out how long people felt it takes a person to grieve. In a survey I took at a local college, 50% of those interviewed felt the length would be two to three weeks, maybe a month. Only those who had lost a person close to them said there was no time limit. How many of us have repressed, or rushed the process just to make others around us happy. We want to have others in our lives doing this time period. However, many leave us. They do not feel comfortable around us like we stated earlier. I don't think we should give in to those who are trying to convince us that we have indeed grieved long enough. How are we going to handle people like this in our lives? We just lost our spouse, and now we must pretend that everything is ok? I don't think so. Unfortunately, I did try and conform to the needs of those around me. I would not do this again. I now know and accept the fact it is ok to cry. It is ok to grieve. Let's remember, God has not set a time limit on our grief. It is good to know that we will not have this feeling forever. Look at Romans 8:18, "I consider that our present sufferings are not worth comparing with the glory that will be revealed in us".

People who are telling us we are grieving too long either have not lost someone close to us or are talking from the standpoint of wanting to make themselves feel better. The way to do this is to try and control how they want us to act or feel. Don't allow others to tell you that it is time for you to stop grieving. They are not walking in your shoes. Perhaps, a simple "I understand that is how YOU feel but, that is not where I am. I am still grieving". It might be necessary go our separate ways from this person for a time period. Some friends and or family members may not feel comfortable being around you. I recall my first Christmas without my Jerry. I was holding my kids and crying. My kids at this time were 11 months and almost two. My dad got right in my face and told me, "Knock it off! Jerry has been gone for over 5 months". Well, I was able to turn off the tears very fast. I put on a smile and pretended that everything was great. Inside I was feeling "How dare you "! I was so mad and hurt. But Praise God, everything was great. Yes, I am being sarcastic. But this is how my life was with my family and most of my friends. Everyone wanted me to be over it. We can't speed up the process like they want us to. Now, some of you may be able to deal with issues more quickly. However, I have found this is not the norm. Yet, there are those who can function the way my dad wanted me to. So, we might want to be mindful of whom we share information. Not everyone will understand what we are going through. Our feelings are of tantamount importance to us, and we should not be discounted for the sake of influencing others to feel better about being around us. How much we can share with a person depends on the strength of the relationship that you have with that person or persons.

Keep a list of phone numbers in your journey handy, so you will be able to call someone in case of an emergency or just for one of those days when you are in need of someone to talk to. Please realize that not everyone will want to chat and therefore confirm with them ahead of time when they will be able to talk if you should need to call. Keep your journal handy also to write your feelings down when someone is trying to put you down or make you feel guilty because they think you are taking too long. Writing your feelings down will be a way of getting your feelings down and not having to repress them. We have talked about how repressing your feelings can cause your emotions to come out in ways that are not always healthy. *Remember, God is with you in your grief as long as it takes. Let's look at a key verse again!*

Hebrews 4:16 "Let us then approach God's throne of grace with confidence, so that we may receive mercy and find grace to help us in our time of need."

We are going to be looking at the 5 stages of grief and how we might experience the stages.

Chapter 7: The Journey of Grief is NOT a Straight Line.

The 5 stages of grief were originally identified by Kubler-Ross as she was working with her terminally ill patients. But an often-overlooked truth about these 5 stages is that you may experience some of the stages multiple times, even though some counselors often use and refer to these steps when supporting the bereaved. However, there are some that will not refer to these stages while working when coming alongside and helping someone who is grieving. We will use them to help us further study the stages of grief and how they will affect us. The stages in chronologically order are denial, anger, bargaining, depression, and acceptance. It is important for us to realize that we may go through some or all these stages several times. The stages of grief and how you may go through them can be determined by how you lost your spouse. Were they terminally ill where you did some of your grieving while they were on hospice or in the process of dying? Did they die a sudden death like my husband did? Is it possible to get to the stage of acceptance and then go back to denial? How are we going to deal with all of this? Will we ever truly accept the fact that our spouse is gone and they are not coming back? We will ever be happy again? Do we have the right to be happy when our spouse had died and left us? One of the most important questions, I think, will I ever stop missing my spouse?

The stages of grief have been widely discussed and even debated in some settings, but I can honestly say that the first stage, denial, was a very very challenging one for me. If you'll remember, at the time of my husband's death, we were stationed in Oxford England. This meant I was away from everything and everyone I know. I felt isolated and really battled depression during this time.

A lot of my depression was due to the fact I had two young children, and I was so far away from my family. We did not live on base and so I was not able to meet any other Air Force people that I could do things with. It was interesting that my husband asked me three weeks before he died what I would do if he passed. And at the time, I didn't want to have such a morbid conversation, but he insisted that I give him an answer. I mentioned the children and I would go back to California, and I would finish my bachelor's degree, all of which he seemed to deem an acceptable response.

Even after having that conversation with Jerry, when it was actually time to make plans for his funeral, it felt surreal. The kids, my mom, and I flew to Indiana because I wanted to have him buried near his mother. When we arrived at the funeral parlor, I can honestly say I was still in denial. I was so deep in this phase of my grief that even as I saw him lying there in the casket, part of me expected him to sit up and say, "Have you learned your lesson?"

But, it actually ended up being more of a reality check that I ever expected.

I started to really understand and let it sink in that he was really gone.

There was no more denying it.

I was officially coming out of denial.

It really took a lot for me to realize and accept that my husband was gone, and you may have had just as difficult of a time navigating denial during your time of grief too. With this in mind, I want to encourage you not to force the process and don't give way to feelings that you are stuck, because it is all part of the process.

In fact, as you grieve, you may find yourself facing the different phases a number of times. Even though I felt myself coming out of denial during the planning and preparation of Jerry's funeral, it came up again the day of his funeral.

After the funeral, as we drove to the cemetery, denial and disbelief became evident again as I found myself in that surreal place once more. I sat next to Jerry's father, still processing everything from emotions, to responsibilities, to fears, then back to emotions. I was struggling, fighting to keep things together as an officer approached to present my father-in-law with an American Flag.

I wanted to cry but I couldn't.

I felt as if I was playing the scene of a widow in a movie. Then when it came time to leave, I broke down and kept screaming, I did not want to leave him. At this moment, I felt a hand firmly grasp my arm, and before I knew it, I was being led back to the car.

It made me feel as if my feelings, my outward expression of my pain was not acceptable.

Family and friends all gathered at the church where we had a light lunch, and even after planning the funeral, attending the funeral, and seeing them lower his casket into the ground, I still excepted, and hoped Jerry would show up.

But he was gone.

And this was slowly sinking in deeper and deeper. The more I navigated through denial. The rawer my emotions were. That's when anger showed up and I realized at that moment that Jerry was really gone.

I looked around and realized that at this repast following the funeral, people were laughing and talking as if it was just another day.

I did my best to "keep up appearances', by smiling, mingling, and looking as if I was in good spirits. But on the inside, anger was brewing.

Just moments ago I was not even allowed to cry out in my grief, and here I was in the midst of friends and family who were supposed to love Jerry and miss him as much as I did.

How could they be so happy?

At that moment, I hated every one of them!

Then to add insult to injury, I realized that someone had begun passing around our wedding pictures. That's when I stormed out of the room to be by myself.

That's when I was finally able to cry.

I had accepted the fact that my Jerry was gone. But my anger went on. After everything that happened that day, I was so angry and lonely that I was thinking about how and when I could kill myself.

I felt truly isolated and hopeless in my grief.

But then a conversation with a friend really helped me and stopped me from taking my life. She knew how I was feeling, and during a phone call, said, "Judy, you have people who love you here; you can't do that!"

While in your grief, it is perfectly normal to feel like you can't or even shouldn't go on, but DO NOT give in to these thoughts and feelings.

Yes, we still grieve. Yes, we miss our spouse and want to be with them.

The devil would love for you to believe that you will never be happy again. But, in Jesus, we do have the victory.

As I think back on my grief journey, I am reminded of a lesson my pastor taught just before I returned to California. The focus of the lesson was simply 'God's Love'. And even in this very painful time, a time when I was on an emotional rollercoaster and feeling alone, I really wanted to believe that God did love me.

But, sadly, I couldn't.

I listened to the teachings and examples laid out by the pastor, and I felt like standing up and calling the pastor a liar. My desire to lay out my own argument got so strong that I had to just leave the sanctuary.

I was fuming that anyone would try and tell me that God loved me.

After that, the pastor came and asked a little about Jerry. He said that Jerry was happier and better off with the Lord. Then he asked me if I was a Christian.

I replied, "Of Course," to which he replied that I would have God to help me through this, and before he left, he prayed, while I sat there pretending to listen.

At that moment, I felt that if God was the kind of God who would just take my husband, then send people to tell me He loved me, I wanted nothing to do with him.

Does this sound familiar?

Here's something that you may not have known or heard before.

It's ok if you're angry with God. It's normal. God knows you are angry, so be honest with Him about how you feel.

The other thing you have to know is that not everyone needs to know that you are angry with God. If you share this with some people, you could have to deal with their belief that you can't or shouldn't feel that way, or even their belief that it's a sin to feel the way you do.

This is not true.

As I noted earlier, God already knows how you feel, so just be honest.

I know this may be easier said than done, and I wish I could tell you that I was angry with God and everyone else, but that was not the case. To be honest, I had so many emotional battles at any given moment during that time, and I again came back to the feeling of not wanting to live anymore.

Why?

The simple answer is that I was tired.

I was tired of life and did not feel it was worth living, and I was tired of so many problems.

So, I decided I was not doing it anymore.

I even went as far as calling a friend to come over and take care of the kids.

And as I sat there with a handful of sleeping pills in one hand and my bible in the other, I

cried out to God, "Give me a verse that shows you exist, or I am done".
I opened my bible to Psalms 14:1 "The fool hath said in his heart there is no God."

I sat with that for a moment. I felt heard, and I found myself thanking God for that.

Then I asked, "Now, give me a reason for going on".

And that's when I was led to Jeremiah 29:11, "For I know the plans I have for you, declares the LORD, plans for welfare and not for evil, to give you a future and a hope."

I sat and cried and thanked God for showing me these two verses. Now, some of you may have done something similar or totally different from what I did, but as I mentioned several times throughout this chapter, being angry with God is very normal and happens to a lot of people who are grieving.

Even today, I consider Jeremiah 29:11 to be my life verse. You may have a favorite verse also that you hold dear to your heart. Use this verse as a means of comfort if you can. I did start to feel better after this night. I had a reassurance without a doubt that God was real, and he had a purpose for my life, even if I wasn't sure of what the purpose was at that time.

Holding on to my faith and finding joy took work. I found myself navigating and cycling through all kinds of emotions as I grieved.

I even went through a period of bargaining.

This was a time when I tied negotiating with God by promising if He brought Jerry back to me, I would go back to England and not be depressed.

So, in addition to dealing with a myriad of emotions, you may find yourself bargaining with God in reference to your spouse's passing.

This is normal.

At the time Jerry died, I was not walking close to God, so I thought that He was punishing me by taking my husband.

How was your relationship with God prior to your spouse's death?

This may impact your experience with the bargaining phase and even times when you blame yourself for the death of your spouse.

For me, these thoughts and feelings persisted for months, and nine months after Jerry's death, I was still blaming myself for Jerry's death and going through counseling.

With the help of my counselors, I was able to establish routines that helped me deal with my feeling and begin to heal.

1. I had always been taught that God's love for me was based on my performance. What a legalistic way to live? I found that God loves me period! There are no strings attached. I found it very hard to grasp the full reality of this and be able to apply it to my life.

2. God is going to be with me in my grief as long as it takes. He has not set down a law saying, "Only one year, and that is all". He wants us to come to him with our hurts and grief.

3. I am not telling people that everything is okay when it's not. I am dealing with each issue of my grief as it comes up and allowing myself to cry if so needed. Before this, most of the time I was denying all my grief and letting it compound.

4. I have learned that the way a person responds to God regarding the loss of a loved one through death is greatly determined by their relationship with Him prior to their death.
5. Most importantly, I have learned to be honest with God about all things. This has made things much easier on me as I continue to work through my grief.

These 5 things helped me to recover from the depression and grief. Then I was in new territory.

Acceptance.

Acceptance, now there's a word we all anticipate happening with our spouse's death. We will all reach this point at different times. Acceptance does not mean that you will not miss them. Of course, you will. They were such a part of your and your children's life. We who are Christians will know we will see them again. But until that time we need to continue our lives. No one said this was going to be easy. But we go on.

We have dealt with a lot in this chapter. We have discussed the different phases of grief. How they affect us differently. Keeping track of your feelings in a journal will help. Also, going to a bereavement support group may be beneficial. Knowing that others understand how you feel and listen to what you are saying without being judgmental is comforting. Get phone numbers from friends that you develop from these groups. It's so beneficial to be able to have someone that you can call that knows how you are feeling. Remember, everyone is different in the grieving process. Don't compare your self to others. In our next chapter we are going to be talking about sudden death and long-term illness. Our relationship with our loved one prior to their death and how this might affect us now.

Chapter 8: Your Relationship With the Person You Lost Significantly Impacts Your Response to God During the Grieving Process

We've been speaking extensively about being angry as it relates to the loss of your spouse, and I want to continue the conversation on anger because it is a genuine AND normal emotion that you can feel daily and as it relates to God. Another layer of anger that you may not expect, but is healthy is the anger you may feel towards the spouse who died.

Regardless of the root or trigger of the anger, in most cases, it is an emotion that we all struggle to handle. And even in our anger, we can find ourselves wondering or worrying about whether or not our spouse ended up in a "better place". The situation can is more challenging if you did not have the chance to say "Goodbye" to your spouse or if the last communication or encounter you had with them was an argument and not being able to say "I'm sorry".

So, let's deal with the emotions and the myriad of questions that can come up during the grieving process like:

- How do I handle not being sure that my loved one is in a better place?
- What is the difference between sudden death and a long term death in terms of how we may grieve?
- Do we handle both of them the same way?
- What steps can we take in the final days with our spouse if they had a long term illness?

And it is essential to realize that the grieving process is very personal and not often a journey that friends and family understand. In fact, and surprisingly, the most common and relatable part of the entire process is the anger towards God. And as common as that feeling is, it ultimately leads us all to a place of despair if left unaddressed. It is truly an age-old story; take the story of David in the bible for example. David felt abandoned by God, something I can relate to because I thought the same way when Jerry died. In David's story, he called out to God for help, he asked to be saved, and he ultimately felt angry and alone.

And in Psalms 22: 1-3, we can see how David responded to God, "My God, my God, why have you abandoned me? Why are you so far away when I groan for help. Every day I call to you, my God, but you do not answer. Every night I lift my voice, But I find no relief. Yet you are holy, enthroned on the praises of Israel."

I wanted to show you that even people in the bible were angry at God.

However you're feeling, let God know. Let Him know the intimate details of your emotions so that He can comfort and guide you. God knows you're angry with him, so don't hide behind your smile pretending that everything is just fine. And in all things remember, repressed anger can cause many other issues to come up in your life.

I honestly believe that my repressed anger after Jerry died led to me being suicidal. With this in mind, communicating with your spouse is another powerful way to deal with your grief.

You read, right?

Talking to your spouse by writing letters or talking to them out loud can keep you from suppressing thoughts, feelings, and emotions. Doing this would also help if you weren't able to say goodbye to your spouse before they passed on, or if you have unexpressed feelings due to an argument.

Now how do we handle not being sure that my loved one is in a better place?

Answering this question can be challenging.

The bible says in John 3:16, "For God so loved the world that he gave his only begotten son that whosoever believeth in him shall not perish but have everlasting life."

If our spouse made this choice and asked Jesus into their life, we have God's promises in this verse that they are spending eternity with Jesus. And, if we also have made the same commitment, then we'll see them again. This is comforting and can help you to reestablish or maintain hope. And it is essential to remember that God is merciful. And some of us have to stand on 2 Peter 3:9, which says, "The Lord is not slack concerning his promise, as some men count slackness; but longsuffering to us-ward, not willing that any should perish, but that all should come to repentance."

Dealing with sudden death comes with its own set of challenges.

My husband died of a brain aneurysm and was found dead on the side of the road.

I had no prep time.
I had no time to plan anything.
I had no time to brace myself or my family.

And after everything was said and done, I sometimes found myself saying, "How dare he leave me in this situation!"

I was facing a difficult situation, and I couldn't help but wonder why God allowed this to happen.

During this time of high emotions and feelings of uncertainty, be mindful of how much and how often you withdraw from friends and family. It is important to remember this because even though there will be times when you need to spend time with God, there will also be times when being around friends and family help you heal through the grief.

If we are dealing with a spouse that we lost, and it was a long term illness, we may have been able to do things ahead of time. We can ask our spouse what their wishes are regarding their funeral. Perhaps they will even want to plan it with you ahead of time. I know to some this may sound morbid, but to others, it will satisfy a sense of providing the family time of ease, so they don't have to deal with the details of the funeral along with everything else they have to do.

Grief will affect all people differently.

So, when we lose our spouse to an illness that they battled for a long time, what other steps besides planning the funeral can we take to get through this?

First, and this applies to all situations of grieving, deal with things as they happen. Avoid ignoring and denying your feelings as much as you can. Make it a day to day, minute by minute practice to let grief run its course.

Even when dealing with health challenges for an extended time, friends and family may not understand or navigate grief in the same way as you. You may have been your spouse's caregiver and support, and that may affect the way that your pain looks. Also, if your spouse was battling a terminal illness, friends and other family members may not understand the depths of your grief.

Despite the situation or whether or not people understand your process, God knows how you feel. Not only does He see that you are hurting, but He is concerned and waiting to help you through it. This verse gives us this promise, Hebrews 4:16, "Let us then approach God's throne of grace with confidence, so that we may receive mercy and find grace to help us in our time of need."

Chapter 9: Grief Doesn't Take the Day Off for Holidays, Family Gatherings, and Special Occasions

I recall the first year after Jerry died, it seemed like I would never get through it because he was such a massive part of my day to day life. From praying with him daily, to how we interacted during the holidays is something I will always remember. And dealing with the hole his passing left required a lot of care and attention that I was not prepared for.

In most cases, the closeness shared with a spouse is hard to describe or encompass in simple terms. And although the effects of losing them will be different for each one of us, the fact remains that no longer having them by our side impacts us, and the feeling of missing them is present no matter how long ago they passed away.

Even as I write this, I remember how hard the first Christmas following Jerry's death was. Everything seemed to remind me that he was gone. But I learned a precious lesson from that time. New traditions that honor the memory of our loved ones can be very powerful additions to how we celebrate different events and holidays throughout the years. Adding new traditions will allow you to be present in the current celebrations and festivities while still honoring your spouse AND acknowledging their importance to you and your family.

It is also important to remember that different holidays and family gatherings can be highly stressful times in normal circumstances, and when you are grieving, the stress can be that much more intense. For example, the first Christmas after Jerry died I found myself surrounded by family, including all my sisters and their husbands. I was holding my two kids (age 11 months & 2 years old) in my lap, and I remember just crying only to have my dad yell out, "Stop your crying," which made me feel guilty for showing my pain. And on a day that is dedicated to having incredible experiences with friends and family, I felt totally alone. So as you are adding new traditions (i.e., moments of prayer, sharing memories, opening a gift in memory of them, adding a special ornament to the tree for them, etc.), wherever possible, make an effort to plan these things in advance to avoid adding stress to yourself as you navigate balancing several emotions and spending time with friends and family.

Another time of celebration that can trigger multiple emotions in the grieving process is birthdays — specifically, Jerry and the kid's birthdays. For instance, on my son, Nathaniel's 1st birthday, he put his face in the cake. And as everyone stood around the table laughing, I cried because all I could think about was how Jerry was missing it. When our daughter, Elicia, turned 2, I repeatedly thought about how proud Jerry would have been of both of his children.

So, birthdays, anniversaries, graduations, and so on, are all milestones that you want to prepare for emotionally. Your normal will be different from a lot of your loved ones. So make a conscious effort to honor how your life has changed. It doesn't have to always be large gestures, but doing something that lets you have the moment and memories you need as you grieve is a great way to support your healing. And this is a lot healthier than pretending not to feel, pretending that everything is fine, and pretending that you are "moving on with your life," as people often advise those who are grieving.

So let's break down some of the tips we covered so you can start planning and taking action. Here are some things that might be of help to you:

1. If you can plan ahead for the Holiday that is approaching, this might prove to be helpful. Hopefully, you will be able to accept your own feelings on this day. Some people around you, as we mentioned earlier, may not understand or even allow you to feel what you are going through. However, allow yourself to cry. And be ok with stepping away from the festivities so you can process how and whatever you need to.

2. Decide ahead of a holiday, like Christmas, if you want to keep on with the same traditions that you had with your spouse or add some new ones.

3. You may want to do something to honor your spouse. For example, donate to one of their favorite charities, buy new Christmas ornament in their honor, etc., as this will help you to ensure your loved one will always be a part of your life. You can even include

children so that even as they leave home, you have established a tradition of remembering your spouse, and they can continue the tradition with their families.

4. Set aside a specific time to share stories and memories of your loved one. Talking about them and filling the festivities with laughter and acknowledgment is a great way to honor them and connect with others in the family who love and miss them too.

I would encourage you, if possible, not to be alone in the first year of the Holiday season as it can be a challenging time. If you don't have family that you can connect with during these times, you might want to consider volunteering somewhere or reaching out to others who are alone as it can be very healing.

While you may find yourself feeling broken or even guilty for trying to celebrate and find cheer during the holidays, I found that by connecting with and talking to other widows in my church, that is something that many who are grieving face. And the key is to in all things, and all situations allow yourself to grieve as necessary, be gentle with yourself, and above all know that God will see you through these difficult times.

Chapter 10: Additional Tools for When Anger and Guilt Resurface.

Throughout the grief process, anger and guilt will be constants that you face. They are both natural parts of the process. Regardless of how many times we see them, dealing with these emotions can be challenging. And if you sprinkle a little bit of denial into the mix, it officially becomes an emotional rollercoaster. But guess what, God still loves us even when we are smack, dab, in the middle of grief.

The cycles of guilt and anger are unpredictable, but when we decide to allow ourselves to grieve fully as needed, it becomes possible to balance the two. And let me say this - regardless of if your anger is towards God, your friends, your family, yourself, or even your spouse, it is manageable.

And this anger is different from your other encounters with anger because the root of it is the pain of losing a loved one you vowed to be with for the rest of your life.

Let me share this with you so you are able to better understand where I am coming from. There were multiple issues in my life as a child that caused me to be angry. Some of these issues followed me into my adult life. I went through physical, emotional, and sexual abuse from my stepfather.

But since losing my husband, I have forgiven my stepdad.

However, as it is for most of us, forgiving does not mean forgetting.

"You will never amount to one G-D thing," are words I heard every single day of my childhood, and I believed this well into adulthood. So, when my husband died, and I found myself deep in anger, depression, and feeling abandoned by God, I went back to the feelings of isolation and abandonment I felt as a child hearing those damaging words from a parent.

While one situation had nothing to do with the other, the mental and spiritual place I was in was the same, which triggered other memories and thoughts that were not helpful or healthy.

What type of anger from your past have you carried over into your adulthood?

Has this anger been compounded by the death of your spouse?

I'm reminded of the night before my husband's funeral. To be honest, I will never forget it. I took a long walk that night. I remember the stars were bright and sparkling. They seemed to be rejoicing that I was in so much pain. During my walk, I spent some time screaming. I was blaming others for the death--- the physician, Jerry, but mostly God. I was very angry! I could hardly see straight. I went to bed around midnight, but I don't think I got to sleep until around 4 am. My anger was so strong when my husband first died. Some of us will not deal with any type of anger until well after the death of our spouse. If we were happy prior to their death, this is most likely going to be the case. So, what is your situation? Are you dealing with anger toward God? The first step is to tell God that you're angry with him. He knows you are angry anyway so talk to Him about it.

I remember talking to God about Jerry's death on and off.

At first, I was not honest about my anger toward him. It took me about five years to get to the point that I was honest. I could no longer play the happy little Christian (mommy, daughter, sister, and friend) that everyone wanted me to be. It got to the point I was so angry that I no longer wanted to stay around. Yes, I was suicidal.

From this point, I put myself in a safe environment by checking into a Christian mental Health facility. My kids lost their dad when they were five months and 18 months. I did not want them to have to grow up knowing daddy died, and mommy killed herself. Those eight weeks in the hospital saved my life. I had dealt a little bit with my anger at God over Jerry's death before my hospital stay. However, it was while I was in the hospital that I saw exactly how angry I was at God. One of the things that helped me deal with this anger was to write a letter to Jerry. In the letter I told him how mad I was at him. I shared how difficult it was for me to raise our kids on my own. I was able to see God's love for me during this time in the hospital. As far as others not helping me, this was hard for me. I had to just accept the fact that some people would not understand my anger. I had to understand that they could not be around me because they didn't feel comfortable with my anger. That was ok. We need to realize that some people just can't handle this. Until they go through a loss, they are not going to be able to understand what we are dealing with. I did go through being extremely angry with God. If you have also, it's normal. God understands and loves you so much. I know you may be feeling God does not love me or he would not have taken my spouse away from me. This is a normal and painful reaction.

Our friends and family should be here for us, right?

Yes, they should, but this is not reality with everyone. As we deal with our anger honestly, we will be able to deal with our grief in a healthy way. God will bring the people into our lives that will help us. Also, God will never leave us. He will be with us as long as it takes for us to work through our anger.

Guilt is another part of grieving. Guilt is another emotion that can be hard to deal with. I felt so guilty when my husband, Jerry, died. There were so many "If only." The night before he died, he had a horrible headache, and his eyes were all red. I should have taken him to the hospital. He called the day he died and told me he had gone to the hospital because of the awful pain in his eyes. I should have told him to go back to the hospital. I had been so depressed while being in England. I felt guilty because I thought God took Jerry home because I was not content while being in England. I felt guilty on the day of the funeral. I was smiling on the outside but fuming on the inside.

I felt guilty because I was not smiling and laughing like everyone else was.

My husband was with the Lord, and that meant that I should have been happy and smiling, right? The answer is NO. I felt even more guilty after the funeral when we went to the house for dinner after the funeral. This is what I wrote in the grief paper I wrote referring to this dinner: "Shortly after the funeral, we all went to Dad's house. People were talking and laughing. On the outside, I was smiling and quite cheerful. On the inside, I was burning with anger. How can they be so happy? I hated every one of them! What really set me off was when someone showed me our wedding picture. I stamped out of the room and upstairs to be by myself".

Dealing with the cycles of guilt, anger, sadness, hopelessness, etc., can be overwhelming, to say the least, when dealing with guilt around the loss of our spouse, some of us may feel overwhelmed. We may have been told, "You don't need to feel guilty." My first thought when I was told that was, "Don't tell me how I should feel. You have no idea of what I have been through".

Our feelings of guilt need to be assessed and validated. It is important to remember just because we feel guilty does not mean we are guilty.

So, how are we going to deal with this emotion called guilt?

Here are some suggestions:

1. Consider what your spouse would say to you about you feeling this way.
    - What would you say to your loved one about your guilt?
    - What would you picture them saying to you?

2. Do something about feeling guilty.

- You might want to share with others about what you've learned about feeling guilty.
- Don't let it consume you.

3. Forgive yourself.
    - We know this is not going to be easy, however.
    - We are not going to forget.
    - We can start the process of moving in a new direction.

4. Are our feelings of guilt based on reality or something that we had no control over?
    - Decide, and then forgive yourself.
    - Access your thoughts about "what could I have done differently," and if it's not based in reality, acknowledge that and talk your way through it.

5. Acknowledge that grief is a normal reaction and ALLOW it!

We have dealt with a lot in this chapter. We all know that anger and guilt are real emotions, and we must deal with them. We have talked about ways to deal with anger and guilt. Another thing I would suggest is journaling. Journaling is a way to deal with our emotions that may not be so easy for us to deal with. It also is a means for us to be able to go back and see how God has been with us in our grief. Be honest in your journaling. We have come a long way in dealing with these two emotions. Be honest with God in how you feel because he already knows. Be selective as to who you share your feelings with. It's ok to respond to people who ask how we are doing with, "I am having a hard time please pray for me."

In the next chapter we're going to take a look at experiences we may face as we grieve and our reactions to them.

Chapter 11: When the Unknown Comes to Light.

The loss of our spouse can bring things into our life that we have not had to deal with yet. For instance, like me, you may now find yourself facing the challenges of being a single parent after your spouse has passed. Dealing with your grief, paying the bills, returning to work, and being the sole provider and caretaker for the children can feel like it all comes crashing down on your shoulders at once.

If you were the one who established the budget, processes, and structure for the household, then you must keep doing it even when you feel like you can't. But if it's all new to you, you have to figure out what works for you so that you can keep things running and in order. You will want to make sure that you collect the necessary paperwork. You will need social security numbers, birth and marriage, and death certificates. You may also need military discharge paperwork and bank account numbers. You will need to contact your health insurance coverage company. You may want to make a list of all your assets, so you have a total for this. It might be a good idea to have a friend or close family member to help you gather all this information and assist you in the process of carrying out each task.

What about the kids?

When Jerry first died, I was overwhelmed in so many ways, and my kids were too young to understand what was happening.

The day after he died, my daughter slept much later than she usually did, and I remember thinking, maybe God had taken her, too. Then the first thing she said when I picked her up was, Daddy, and all I could tell her was that "Daddy went bye-bye."

My son was an infant, so he had no concept of what was happening.

As the kids got older, I had to deal with my grief and theirs.

One way I dealt with their grief was by taking them back to Indiana, where their father was born. Together, we saw the house that he was born in, we visited the High School he went to, my sister-in-law took us around to various places he used to hang out, and the last thing we did was visit his grave.

Seeing their dad's name on the grave was very hard for all three of us, but it was also a time for all of us to celebrate Jerry's life. And as time went on and we faced the challenges around weddings and graduations, we had these moments to reflect on. We also openly communicated about how we imagined things would be if he had been with us.

You, too, will have things happen as your children grow up. Like I mentioned earlier, if your children are older, you may have to deal with their grief and yours. Another issue that may be hard for you and your children is the lack of influence of not having either a Dad or Mom role model as they are growing up.

I was fortunate to have one of my pastors spend some time with my son through the years. Perhaps, someone from your church or circle of friends will be able to help you out if you are in this situation. I know this is not an easy request for some. Having a married man do this might be hard because the wife may get jealous or feel threated by you. I know this may seem silly, but it is a reality of what may happen. Take the time to pray about this and see what God will provide.

What are some of the ways we can help our children through grief?

Here are a few suggestions you may want to use:

1. Some parents think that not talking about death is in the best interest of the child. However, just the opposite is true.
   - Children must be allowed to talk about their feelings that are related to the one they have lost.
   - When they are talking, don't interrupt them or try to correct something they are saying because this is not the time for correction but a time for active listening.
   - If they aren't allowed to talk about it, the process of healing will be harder.
   - Allowing them to talk about it is also important because it is setting a foundation for how they might deal with other loses throughout their life.
2. It's important for children to know we're listening. (Eye contact is an easy way to let them know you're listening).
   - This may mean sitting down in two chairs facing each other.

- Or, you as the adult get on their knees so that they are eye level with the child.

3. Let the child know it is ok to be sad and cry. It is ok for children to see we also miss the person by our tears and sadness.

4. Be sure and demonstrate an attitude of caring that lets the child know they will not be judged for what they are sharing.

5. Just like us adults, there is no time frame for children as they are grieving. Birthdays, holidays, family gatherings may be a hard time for children. Of course, this will depend on the age of the child and the relationship of the loss.

6. Children also will go through a time of shock and denial at the beginning of the grieving process.

7. Children may also show various behavioral issues that were not present before the death of a parent. Realize this is normal.

Consider consulting a Children's counselor if further assistance is needed.

After you navigate all the different levels of your new normal, there may come a time down the road where you wonder if you should ever get married again.

This is a question that has a different answer for each one of us.

For others it may spawn more questions like:

- Were we happily married with our first spouse?
- Are we trying to find someone to fill the shoes of our deceased spouse?
- Did we have a married relationship that we were relieved to get away from?

For Widows and Widowers considering remarriage, here are some things you may want to consider.

One of the most important things you need is to be sure that you are guided by is the scripture.

How long should we wait to remarry is a question that each of us will consider?

If the death of your spouse was due to a long term illness, you most likely would have done some grieving before their death, and you may feel comfortable remarrying sooner. If the loss of your spouses was sudden, like mine, you might want to wait for a more extended period to ensure that you are progressing through grief. If there are children involved, take the time to introduce them to your potential new spouse. It may be hard for your children to have a new Mom or Dad in their life. Allow them to express their feelings regarding this. You and anyone you bring into the lives of you and your children should thoroughly discuss child-rearing to determine if your goals for discipline and other issues on parenting are in alignment with each other. And if a difference of opinion exists, is it possible to compromise.

Don't allow grief and missing your spouse to move you into remarrying prematurely.

If you are considering a serious relationship or marriage, make sure you talk about money.

It would be highly advisable to establish and agree upon checking, savings, and various other accounts as to how these funds would be used. You may want to enlist the help of a pastor or a close mutual friend to help you with this. New wills and/or trusts should be established. You may want to have a prenuptial agreement. If one of you were to pass away, this would make it so much easier for those left behind.

Are your religious beliefs compatible? Make all efforts to resolve this in detail. It would be hard to establish resolutions regarding this once you're married. How often do you go to church? What are your practices regarding tithing? It's not a good assumption for us to think our spouse will change and follow our practices regarding this.

The bible makes it very clear we are not to be "unequally yoked" with a nonbeliever (2 Corinthians 6:14) KJV "Do not be unequally yoked together with unbelievers. For what fellowship has righteousness with lawlessness? And what communion has light with darkness." For the believer do not enter a marriage thinking you will win your spouse to accept the gospel truths. Follow God's lead and obey this verse.

Where will you live? Will you stay in your house or move into theirs? Will you buy or rent a new place? You might sell both of your houses. Will you use some of their furniture and some of yours. Or will you buy new furniture? This is something that you must discuss ahead of time.

Talk together to come to an agreement that will satisfy both of you.

You will never find a mate to replace your first one. Your new spouse will have some good and bad qualities, just like your first one did. Try not to make comparisons either direct or indirectly about your first spouse to your new one. What happened in your first marriage is in the past, let it stay there.

How will you handle holidays and family traditions? There are many factors to take into consideration here. Try and keep as many of your old family traditions as possible. What new ones will you and your spouse like to start together? You must be willing to compromise with this. Your traditions can not be the same way they were with your first spouse. Because you've taken the time to plan together, your family gathering can be fun-loving for all.

Who did all the bill paying with the first marriage? If you were the one taking care of this, then continuing it may be hard but attainable. If you're not the one who did this, you will have to be gentle with yourself as you process all that needs to take place to start this journey. Here is a list of paperwork that is suggested:

1. Social security numbers
2. Birth certificate
3. Marriage certificate
4. About 25 copies of the death certificate (you will need copies for various things)
5. Bank account numbers
6. Health insurance information
7. Make a list of all your assets
8. Life insurance

It would be advisable to have someone help you with this. Dealing with your grief and all of this can become overwhelming. But it is important that paperwork is kept up to date as needed so that all will be in a good legal position. Please be prepared for when you receive your life insurance check. This can be overwhelming. Seeing that insurance check often means knowing, "They really are gone." I know that I had a very hard time with this.

We have dealt with how to handle our own grief and help our children through their grief. We have reaffirmed the fact that there is no time frame on grief. We were able to look at some of the reasons to remarry and some things to consider together before we take that step. In our next chapter, lets share and talk about what is helpful or unhelpful in the loss of a spo

Chapter 12: Don't Fear Grief; Just do the Work to Heal

We have talked about various aspects on how to cope after the loss of a spouse. I want to close this book by sharing what is helpful and what isn't when dealing with the loss of a loved one.

You may be asking, why does God allow pain?

I know, because I asked the same thing. And then I realized that I had always been taught that God's love for me was based on my performance.

What a legalistic way to live.

But as I matured in my relationship with God, I grew in the wisdom that He loves me, period!

AND, there are no strings attached.

It took a while for me to grasp the full reality of this and apply it to my life. But as a result of continuously working on myself and my relationship with God, I am confident that even in my times of grief, He is with me. He has not written a law that says He's there for me to grieve for only one year; in fact, he wants me to come to him with my heartache and grief.

I don't tell others how to grieve OR allow others to tell me how to grieve, and I've learned the way that a person responds to God regarding the loss of a loved one is impacted by their relationship with their loved one before their death.

And above all things, I have learned and decided to be honest with God no matter what, which has made it much easier on me as I continue to work through my grief.

As I share this, I am reminded of a letter I received from a friend that read:

"Judy, I just want to encourage you as you have had such a hard struggle writing the paper about grief. I know it has been hard to go over all the feelings of suffering, anger, loss, and the memories of people who did destructive things and your own ups and down in the midst of all that" He went on to say *"As I have been with you in part of what you've been through it has helped me to grow and have more understanding and be*

more effective in teaching others how to minister to people in grief. So, I want to thank you for helping me to grow" The next part of this letter helped reconfirm my own discovery that God will be with me as long as my grief takes "I also have a message from the Lord to you. "Judy, I care for you; I know your burden is heavy, I will continue to be with you and help you bear the burden. I will never leave you or forsake you". He finished his letter with "Judy, I send you a message of greeting, warmth, love, support, and understanding. Our prayers continue to be on your behalf. Your brother and sister in Christ."

This note could not have come at a better time. Messages of concern and love to a person who is going through grief are essential and cherished. By sharing this, perhaps it will help on your journey.

Here's what I found helpful during my time of grief:

1. Having a friend who listens and wipes away my tears.
2. Being encouraged as I worked my way back into a normal routine (like going back to school).

3. Notes, especially handwritten ones, have been very helpful.
4. People calling me on the phone to check in on me or chat.
5. A circle of accepting friends to reach out to when I was having a bad day.
6. Someone to point me back to what God said in His word and remind me that God will be with me in my grief – as long as it takes.
7. The physical presence of a friend is comforting.

Here were some of the things that didn't help me. (Perhaps you can relate to them.)

1. Being told to "stop wallowing in my sorrow."
2. Being told that "Jerry was better off with the Lord; he belonged to Him anyway."
3. Being told, "I was not the only one with problems."
4. Being told to reach out if I needed people when they didn't mean it.

There are several reasons that God allows us to face heartache, some of which I was introduced to during a bible study I attended. And as I dealt with Jerry's death, I was better able to understand each one.

Sometimes we endure suffering:

1. For our growth.
2. To induce us to obey, to call us back to him.
3. To build endurance and dependence on Him.
4. To show us His plan for our life.
5. To learn to trust God when bad things happen.
6. One person said theologically pain causes growth.

Compared to some, my view of suffering is limited. In reflecting on the first year after my husband's death, I would not say that God allows suffering as punishment. If that were true, we would all be dead within the next five minutes because of what we deserve.

But I can see God's work in my life.

And with the right tools and support, I have been able to flourish and grow even after experiencing the unexpected loss of my husband. I have gone to a bereavement support group, I realized how much God loves me, I know He wants me to come to Him with my heartache, I am positioned to help others based on my experiences. By consistently acknowledging my progress through grief I can now allow myself to be happy, and above all, I seek Gods guidance in everything.

My prayer for every person who reads this book is that by sharing my life and experiences on my grief journey, your hope is replenished, and you can start your life over. I desire to be a reminder to each reader that God is with us through and in ALL things. And I want you, the reader, to know that I am praying for you daily.

May God richly bless your life as you trust him in all your future endeavors.

And remember that God has a promised plan for you and your life.

~Jeremiah 29:11 - *"For I know the plans I have for you declares the LORD, plans to prosper you and not harm you, plans to give you a future and a hope."*

About the Author

Judy St. Pierre is a widow and mother of two, who earned her B.A. in 1985 from Los Angeles Baptist College, which is now the Master's University and worked in the field of education for 27 years.

Today, Judy lives in Rosamond, California, where she is a Volunteer chaplain at Antelope Valley Hospital in Lancaster, California, a substitute teacher and author. She has a heart for people and is currently working to connect with groups, organizations and individuals to share her story and message of dealing with grief, to help others heal faster and more effectively.

Stay Connected

Facebook: https://www.facebook.com/judy.a.pierre

Email: **goodgriefJS@gmail.com**

To connect with Judy or book her to speak.

www.wordtherapypublishing.com

"A Message That Heals"

www.ingramcontent.com/pod-product-compliance
Lightning Source LLC
LaVergne TN
LVHW011426080426
835512LV00005B/287